A Day in the Life of a Colonial Schoolteacher

Kathy Wilmore

Newbridge Educational Publishing

To Bryan Brown, for the encouragement, humor, and grace that helped so much as I wrote this book—and to my mother, Julia C. Wilmore, who got me started.

Published in 2000 by The Rosen Publishing Group, Inc.
29 East 21st Street, New York, NY 10010

Printed by Bang Printing.
Manufactured in Brainerd, MN USA
August, 2012
Rosen PO# 082412Bnb
Sundance/Newbridge PO# 510508

Distributed to the School Market by
Newbridge Educational Publishing.
33 Boston Post Road West, Suite 440
Marlborough, MA 01752
1-800-867-0307

First Edition

Book design: Danielle Primiceri

Photo Credits: Cover, title p., p. 8 © Tate Gallery London/ET Archive, London/Superstock; p. 4 © Superstock; pp. 7, 15, 16, 20 © Archive Photos; p. 11 © CORBIS; p. 12 © City Art Museum of St. Louis/Superstock; p. 19 © The Granger Collection, New York.

Wilmore, Kathy.
A day in the life of a Colonial schoolteacher / by Kathy Wilmore.
p. cm.— (The library of living and working in Colonial times)
Includes index.
Summary: Describes a day in a Colonial American dame school, including who attended, what they learned, and what chores they did.
ISBN 978-1-58273-638-9
1. Education-—United States-—History-—17th century—Juvenile literature. 2. Education-—United States-—History—18th century—Juvenile literature. 3. Teachers—United States—History—17th century—Juvenile literature. 4. Teachers—United States—History—18th century—Juvenile literature. 5. Dame schools—United States—History 17th century—Juvenile literature. 6. Dame schools—United States—History—18th century—Juvenile literature. [1. Schools—History.] I. Title. II. Series.
LA206.W55 1999
370'.973—dc21
98-31953
CIP
AC

Abigail Beech and her school are fictional, but the details in this story about Colonial schoolteachers and Colonial life are true.

CPSIA Compliance Information: Batch #CR114140: For Further Information contact Rosen Publishing, New York, New York at 1-800-237-9932

Contents

Colonial America

Like other Colonial women, Abigail Beech found life in America to be an adventure. People from England began moving to America in the early 1600s to form **colonies**. Mrs. Beech, like many other **colonists**, had come to find a better life for herself and her family. She had no idea that the colonists would later go to war with the English government, or that on July 4, 1776, the United States would become an **independent** country.

The Pilgrims, early colonists from England, arrive in Massachusetts.

The Teacher

Abigail Beech and her husband moved to America from England when they were a young couple. Her husband opened a shoe shop in Connecticut. Like many Colonial shopkeepers, Mr. Beech lived with his family in the rooms upstairs from the shop.

Mrs. Beech ran a school in her home. Since most people in town knew Mrs. Beech, they were happy to send their children to her school.

Many Colonial children had lessons at their teacher's house.

The Students

In most Colonial classrooms, students were usually six to eight years old. There were more boys than girls. Few students were wealthy. Families with a lot of money usually hired **tutors** for their children.

Most families depended on their children to help with work on farms or in shops. That left little time for school. Many parents thought that knowing how to read and do **arithmetic** was important though, so they sent their children to school as often as possible.

◀ ***Colonial children went to school only when their parents did not need them to work at the family farm or shop.***

The School

The school that Mrs. Beech ran was called a **dame** school. Dame schools were usually set up in a teacher's home. Teachers, who were usually older women, often held classes in the kitchen. They could cook or do chores while students did their lessons.

A large Colonial town might also have had a common school. A common school was a one-room schoolhouse. Students were older than dame-school students and most were boys. Common-school teachers were usually men.

Students and teacher at a dame school. ▶

Starting the School Day

Colonial students started the day very early. First they had to do chores at their family's farm or shop. Then they went to school, which started at seven A.M. They usually attended school every day but Sunday.

In winter, children brought wood for the teacher's fireplace. This was part of how parents paid the women who taught their children.

The children sat on wooden chairs or benches while they learned their lessons.

◀ ***Colonial students at a one-room schoolhouse.***

What the Teacher Taught

Most Colonial schools taught at least one basic subject, which was reading. Many of the early **settlers** were very religious. They believed that everyone should be able to read the Bible. Knowing how to write or do arithmetic was important to them, but not as important as reading. Mrs. Beech, like most teachers of the time, taught her students the alphabet and simple words. Then they practiced by reading prayers or rhymes.

Learning to read was a Colonial student's most important task.

+ Aabcdefghijklmnopq
rfstuvwxyz& aeiou
ABCDEFGHIJKLMNOPQ
RSTUVWXYZ
a e i o u
ab eb ib ob ub
ac ec ic oc uc
ad ed id od ud
a e i o u
ba be bi bo bu
ca ce ci co cu
da de di do du
In the Name of the Father, and of the
Son, and of the Holy Ghoſt. Amen.
OUR Father, which art in
Heaven, hallowed be thy
Name; thy Kingdom come, thy
Will be done on Earth, as it is in
Heaven. Give us this day our
daily Bread; and forgive us our
Treſpaſſes, as we forgive them
that treſpaſs againſt us: And
lead us not into Temptation, but
deliver us from Evil. Amen

School Supplies

Colonial classrooms were very simple. They had no blackboards or chalk. Few had books, paper, or pencils.

A hornbook was a flat, wooden board with a handle. It often had the alphabet and numbers carved into one side. A piece of paper with a prayer and a poem written on it was attached to the other side. A thin sheet of animal horn protected the paper from wear and tear.

◀ ***A Colonial hornbook was used by students to help them learn how to read.***

How the Teacher Taught

Mrs. Beech taught many lessons by **reciting** rhymes to her students. They repeated what she said until they had **memorized** it. Mrs. Beech had a different rhyme for each letter in the alphabet. She held up a hornbook and pointed to the letter D. Then she said, "A Dog will bite a thief at night." Then she pointed to E and said, "An Eagle's flight is out of sight." The children repeated each rhyme until they remembered it and knew which letter went with it.

This Colonial teacher from Pennsylvania helps his students with a lesson.

DUNCE

Discipline

Like most Colonial teachers, Mrs. Beech expected her students to study hard and behave themselves. A child who could not answer a question correctly had to sit in the corner wearing a tall, pointy cap that said **DUNCE** on it. Children who forgot to bring firewood in winter had to sit farthest from the fireplace.

Many Colonial schoolteachers were **strict**. A child who misbehaved was hit with a twig or cane, or locked in a closet.

◀ ***This boy's punishment for answering a question incorrectly is having to wear a dunce cap.***

Ending the School Day

Students attended a dame school for two years. Many never went to school again after that. Some studied on their own.

The school day ended at four or five P.M. At the end of the day, the students said a prayer. Then Mrs. Beech sent them home. The children had farmwork or shop work to do before bedtime.

Web Sites:

Due to the changing nature of Internet links, PowerKids Press has developed an online list of Web sites related to the subject of this book. This site is updated regularly. Please use this link to access the list: www.powerkidslinks.com/llwct/dlcteach/

Glossary

arithmetic (uh-RITH-muh-tik) Basic math skills such as adding and subtracting.

colonist (KAH-luh-nist) A person who lives in a colony.

colony (KAH-luh-nee) A group of people who leave their own country to settle in another land but still remain under the rule of their old country.

dame (DAYM) A woman in charge of a household, or an older woman of some importance.

dunce (DUNS) A person who is slow to learn.

independent (in-dih-PEN-dint) To be free from the control, support, influence, or help of others.

memorize (MEH-muh-ryz) To learn something by heart.

recite (re-SYT) To say or repeat aloud.

settler (SEHT-lur) A person who moves to a new land to live.

strict (STRIKT) When someone makes sure that other people follow their rules very carefully.

tutor (TOO-tur) A person hired to give private lessons.

Index